Develop Your Vision Into Practicality

*How to Grow Your Corporate,
Organization, Leadership, Political,
Government or Church Vision!*

Akosuah Appiah Sumney, Ph.D.

DEVELOP YOUR VISION INTO PRACTICALITY
How to Grow Your Corporate, Organization, Leadership, Political, Government or Church Vision!

© **2016, by *Akosuah Appiah Sumney, (BAHR, MAML, Ph.D)***

Forwarded by: Dr. Ray Parker

All rights reserved. No part of this book may be reproduced or transmitted in any form, or by any method, electronic or mechanical, without written permission of the author.

ISBN: 978-0-9971285-1-2

Printed in the United States of American by Parker Books Publishing, Palm Bay, Florida 32909

**Visit our web site for additional information:
http://www.rayparker.net**

For more information contact:

Dr. Akosuah Appiah Sumney

Global Dominion Television: *Africa*
Mission Africa Incorporated
Spintex Highway, Spintex Road (Near Coca Cola Roundabout)

or
BOX 18162
International Airport
Accra Ghana West Africa
0554116401/0543197995

Global Dominion Television: USA
Mission Africa Incorporated
B0X 7175
Moreno Valley
Ca. 92552
9514029877
Social media: Drakosuahsumney
www.missionafricainc.org

DEDICATION

To my parents:

My mother who never went to school but worked tirelessly to train us with at least a college education.

My dad, who served as a government worker made just enough money for the family, but was determined to support all his children to college level of education.

To my husband:
With such a limited support of resources to continue college, yet you came up with such an incredible vision for thousands to follow.

ACKNOWLEGEMENTS

Over a period of six years, I had taken over six hundred Americans from California to Africa for humanitarian, mission work and projects. At the same time, I started to work on a Master's Degree in Management Leadership. I found it very necessary then to upgrade myself in order to lead the teams that were available to me. Many of you were highly educated with Master's degrees and PhD's yet you found me qualified to train and lead you for all those years. My gratitude is to every person among the over one thousand people that I have led from the USA to Africa in ten years. You inspired me to do more and more daily. Leadership challenges instilled in me by you all has been a blessing.

Many of you encouraged and challenged me with the practical assignments that awaited my coming degree. Thanks for the students from Azusa Pacific University, Jackson State University, University of California San Bernardino and University of California Los Angeles (UCLA). When I was invited to lead the schools' teams to Africa, it was a major leadership vision assignment. My encounter with some of the professors from Jackson State University, like Dr. Sabir helped me with my result base approach assignments

Many thanks to Dr. Pamela Christian, Vice Provost for Inclusion and Cross-Cultural Engagement, Biola University who has been very supportive and resourceful to me since the first day I met her. Some of the projects taken with her during this writing on the humanitarian and educational trips to Ghana, made me feel more challenged.

My sincere gratitude to many of you who gave me the encouragement and support to excel in my vision. I want to thank Dr. Reginald Woods of life Changing Ministries for providing encouragement, recommendation and support to me. Mrs. Charlyn Singleton you have been helpful in my thoughts for your boldness to go back for your Master's Degree. That motivated me to go back to school to get a Master's Degree, I admire your grace.

I cannot forget one of my professors, Dr. Ray Parker who graciously led me to the completion of my Degrees; my Master's Thesis and PhD dissertation. You ignited my interest in the topic of Leadership, Management and Human Resources. You also instilled in me that my Master's Degree Thesis and Project work can actually be a book; thanks a million.

This book does not represent the author alone, many ideas were glazed from my professors at Trinity College and Seminary in Indiana. My greatest appreciation however is reserved for my family; my children and my husband who lovingly supported my journey to explore the latest developments in leadership. I know many times my family was used as exploration toward my leadership assignments.

Finally my gratitude to Yahweh, Elohim, through His Son Yeshua, for showing me that there is a purpose in my life. You birthed the vision in me and I dedicate it back to you.

Table of Contents

PREFACE i
INTRODUCTION iii
FOREWORD vi
I. CHAPTER ONE 1
    A. MEANING OF VISION 1
    B. YOUR PERSONALITY 3
II. CHAPTER TWO 5
    A. WHAT A VISION IS 5
    B. BENEFITS OF DEVELOPING A VISION 7
    C. THE IMPORTANCE OF A VISION TO ANY LEADERSHIP, MINISTRY OR ORGANIZATION 12
III. CHAPTER THREE 15
    A. THE PROCESS OF DEVELOPING A VISION 15
    D. MAKING YOUR VISION REALITY 15
    C. THE LEADER'S ROLE IN BIRTHING THE VISION 17
IV. CHAPTER FOUR 21
    A. IMPLEMENTATION OF THE VISION 21
    B. SHARED VISION 23
    C. SOME GREAT VISIONARIES 25
V. CHAPTER FIVE
    A. VISION STATEMENT 28
    B. MISSION STATEMENT 31
    C. CORE VALUES 34

VI. CHAPTER SIX
- A. COMMUNICATING YOUR VISION 36
- B. GREAT LEADERS COMMUNICATE THEIR VISION 39

VII. CHAPTER SEVEN 48
- A. MAKING YOUR VISION A REALITY 48
- B. PERFORMING THE WORK 49

VIII. CHAPTER EIGHT 51
- A. DO NOT ABANDON YOUR VISION 51
- B. VISION AUGMENTATION 52

IX. CHAPTER NINE 54
- A. CONCLUSION 54
- B. POLITICAL TRANFORMATIONAL LEADERSHIP 54
- C. LEADERSHIP AND ORGANIZATIONAL VISION. 57
- D. WISE SAYINGS BY DR. AKOSUAH APPIAH SUMNEY 58

BIBLIOGRAPHY I

PREFACE

"The only thing that can help a visionary succeed is to never lose faith in his vision. - Akosuah Appiah Sumney," - PhD

Before a vision can become a reality it must begin to be articulated in spoken words of confidence. Visions verbalized in words of faith, releases the creativity to bring into existence that which was not. Success is a process, if you ever stop going for it, then you stop being successful. Success is like staircase, one step builds on the former step while preparing for the next step. You cannot go to a new height without being willing to risk it all. I rather attempt something great and fail than not do anything at all. Success is birthed by a great vision.

Vision is the period at which thinking about your work. This is just as essential as constructing your work. In other words, you need to spend time reflecting about your ideas and how they can be crafted into reality to last a long time. Just creating and forming new ideas will not allow you to express your vision. Reflection, reproduction and building has to take place. Critical Thinking has to take place alongside plans of implementation.

A large part of the process of developing your vision takes place without a paper in hand. It doesn't even have to happen where you meditate and think deeply that you have nothing to write on. It can happen wherever you have time to think, in a place that is quiet and conducive to reflection and where you are not distracted by anything. In a way you have to engage in critical thinking about your work. You have to think about what you have done so far and about what you want to do next. You also need to think about what inspired you to start creating that vision in the first place.

TARGET AUDIENCE
The primary target audience for this book is practicing human resources professionals, leadership in organizations, politicians, pastors and the clergy, students and everybody that requires a vision as measuring tape to life. Critical thinking is also about thinking differently. It is about thinking of solutions and possibilities that have not been thought of previously. In many ways, being creative is synonymous with thinking differently. To think differently you have to think differently from "something." You can't think in the immaterial, without some point of reference, some point

when you heard that inner voice saying, this is what you can create, some school of thought to guide you.

    Creating a vision cannot be done in a vacuum. To develop your vision you must take into consideration both what you want to do and what has already been done by other visionaries. Something is different only if it has not been done before, or if it has not been done the way you are doing it. This means that you have to know where you are coming from, what your point of reference is, what your roots are, who your colleagues are, and who is working in the same style as you. In short, you need to know where you fit in.

INTRODUCTION

My vision to become a doctor was since I was a kid. My parents didn't have enough money to pay my way through university though I was very brilliant. I lived in hopefulness that one day I will be able to fulfil my dream to have a Ph.D. It took very long for me to work hard on my own but that dream has been accomplished. After years of being in college and different universities, it has paid off. I never stopped dreaming about that incredible day, it seemed very long and impossible but I have achieved it.

Everybody has a vision or a desire to do something but the question is, how many people are fulfilling their vision? It takes so much courage and boldness to develop a vision into reality. Some dream early in age, say in their teenage years, only to see that vision develop in the later part of their age.

Many are those who have dreamt to establish different things but never were able to bring them into reality. The skeleton of the vision sometimes become so scary that it can be boxed into a secret place without developing it. Get up now and be excited about your vision. It is better you attempt to develop it and fail many times than not doing it at all.

"Vision" is crucial to any leadership, government, ministry or organization... Leaders must be able to articulate clear direction of where they are going, to attempt a business without a clear, well-articulated vision is to invite "stagnant effort".

Deep down within every one of us is a need to make our lives count. Without a vision, life is boring and full of routine. People perish due to lack of a vision, but with a vision, life becomes exciting; every day is a new adventure. With a vision people not only tackle the impossible but accomplish it. Without a vision, little worthwhile is ever attempted. Good things do not happen by chance. Vision is very important, people without a vision cannot even survive let alone thrive. It is a vision that adds excitement and enthusiasm to the life of people.

Vision is the talent of seeing what is invisible and what is hiding from others

The focus of this book will not only be on people in ministry but people in all-round leadership including politicians and students. Developing your vision is as important as starting a business, if not more important. Vision serves as a map; its absence can create a lot of confusion. "Business might do well instantaneously and churches might grow from the beginning, but without a clear vision they shrink or die sooner or later".

I believe that all successful leaders have a vision for their businesses, projects or teams. In fact, you would not be a leader if you did not have a vision, or could not see exciting possibilities in your product or services.

Vision can be seen as a key foundation on which any leadership, church or business must be built.
It is one of many concepts that have a great impact on any organization. The others are core values, mission and strategy. All these relate to one another.
Transferring passion from subject to equipment is not the only reason why we move away from our vision. There are many other events that can cause this to happen. Life has a way of taking us away from what we originally intended to do and to make us do things because we have to, rather than because we want to.
If this sounds familiar you are not alone. This is a common situation that many visionaries face. The way out of it is to first accept it for what it is. Don't refute the facts; just accept them. Then, this being out of the way, go back in time in your mind and remind yourself of the reason why you started the leadership role, the organization or the ministry, in the first place, way back when.
You may be able to do so simply by thinking about it and by remembering events that took place a long time ago. You may also have to go back through your archives so to speak, or make a trip to the place where your first work began to take a look at your first love you created when you just started.

Vision becomes very important once it has been recognized. A lot of work must be put in to bring it to fulfillment. I believe that another aspect of leadership as it pertains to business management is the necessity of business leaders to have a strong vision for their companies and develop winning strategic plans to accomplish organizational objectives.

In this BOOK, these items will be looked at:

- The importance of a vision to any leadership, ministry or organization
- The definition of the word "vision"
- The process of developing a vision
- Communication of the vision
- Implementation of the vision
- Effectiveness of the vision by measurement

Men and women of vision and dreams have no trouble with drifting and laziness because they know where they are going. They find themselves setting measurable, realistic, motivating, and attainable goals though not easy goals that don't challenge their faith. It all begins with a vision! Tell me your vision and I will tell you your future. Take the limit off your mind so that you can allow faith to set in. Get a clear cut picture of the vision in your mind. The core values of the business will be identified. Approaches towards developing and communicating vision in order to realize the importance of creating a strong sense of vision for your organization will also be established.

FOREWORD

In Develop Your Vision into Practicality, Dr. Akosuah Appiah Sumney has drawn together basic ideas from the standard works on leadership theory, ventilated this imposing structure with adequate illustrations and examples, and then added some inspiring and challenging innovative suggestions of her own. When you complete this volume, your insights into vision development, communication, implementation, and preservation will have increased for practical application.

For persons already engaged in Christian management, supervision, and leadership, Dr. Sumney provides the answers to several motivational questions. For example: What is vision? How can vision be developed? How can vision be implemented? How can a vision statement be crafted? How can vision be communicated? How can vision become reality? How can vision be preserved? Not content with being merely theoretical, the author includes at every possible point some helpful "how to do it" advice.

For pastors, Christian leaders, or students of management and leadership theory who recognize the growing importance of vision, this book will be a gold mine of insights and new ideas.

Written not out of the ivory tower of academia but from considerable personal experience and bedrock research, Develop Your Vision into Practicality may well become an outstanding source of facts, inspiration, and motivation for years to come.

Ray L. Parker, PhD
Vice President for Academic Affairs
Master's International University of Divinity
Evansville, Indiana

I. CHAPTER ONE
A. MEANING OF VISION

Vision is the art of seeing the invisible. In this respect, vision is not just "sight." Instead, vision is **insight.** It is the ability to see something that only the visionary can see, something that others do not see because it does not have a physical reality. It is something seen in the mind's eye, something that exists in imagination, something that is within oneself. Finding and expressing one's vision can be a challenging process. Because vision is something that is invisible to others, it is a process that one has to go through essentially by oneself.

Vision is a concise statement or description of the direction in which an individual, group, or organization is headed. Captivating visions, provide people with a sense of purpose, courage and commitment. Followers achieve more and make more ethical decisions when they pursue a worthy goal. To be compelling, a vision must be both desirable and attainable. Uninspiring or unachievable visions are ineffective and may demoralize followers.

When I say 'vision' I'm referring to a plan for a desired result.

Vision – *know where you're going and why*
Communication – *explain the vision clearly in terms of what, why, and how*
Execution – *getting to the desired goal*

Each piece is vital, but in my experience, the most challenging part is communicating the vision in a way that people *hear, understand, and support* it.

Identifying, developing and communicating a clear vision is one of the most important functions any business leader can achieve. This is because it is profitable for all business leaders to understand the basic elements of visioning and how to communicate a clear vision to both employees and customers. Any successful endeavor requires a vision. It will be difficult at first, but with time, it will become successful if kept in its proper perspective.

During this research, these questions will be answered:
- How vital is vision to any organization, leadership or ministry?
- What does the term vision mean?

- Who in the organization, leadership or ministry is responsible for birthing the vision? Vision is defined as "the power which shapes meaning for the people of an organization".

A vision is the ability, or the God-given gift, to see those things which are not, as becoming a reality.

Vision demands an unwavering commitment, it also demands that one can back up this commitment with work because only through work will vision be shared with others.

This study explores the definition of leadership and then goes on to discuss one of the most important functions business leaders perform pertaining to business planning. That critically important function is to develop and create a clear vision for all participants in the business. To sell your creation or brand, you need a vision.

A vision is a picture of the future we seek to create, described in the present tense, as if it were happening now. It shows where we want to go, and what we will be like when we get there. The word comes from the Latin "videre", "to see." "To develop your insights"

When you work on your vision, consider these items:
- Your strategic focus
- Your market place competitive advantage
- What makes you unique and marketable
- How you add value to others
- What are your current competencies
- What are your deeply felt values

In this book, I am giving you simple steps to identify where you are and to articulate your vision to position your future direction.

Developing a clear and effective vision provides many benefits to the business. Not only does a clear, shared vision help define the values of the company and its employees, but it also helps guide the behavior of all employees. A strong vision also leads to productivity and efficiency. A vision provides a driving force. It is clear, specific and simple. One should be able to easily incorporate it, apply it to all decision making, articulate it without having to read the text, and act upon it.

Developing a strong vision requires an acknowledgement, development and understanding of core values that the business holds. Once the business manager identifies the core values of the business, he or she needs to effectively articulate and communicate the purpose and envisioned future of the business".

With such a clearly communicated vision, the business will simplify things for its employees and create a sense of shared vision.

This book will explore the importance of vision and creativity in order to help politicians, leaders, pastors and business managers lead their own organizations more effectively.

B. YOUR PERSONALITY

An artist's work is given form and style by his personal vision. It is not solely technique, but the way he looks at life and the world around him. Developing a Vision for your work is presenting to others, through your personal observations, what you see in your mind's eye. It is therefore about you. It is about how you see the world, about what you see that others do not see, and about your emotional response to the high lights that you picture. In many ways it is about your personality.

In the process of developing this vision you must be yourself and display your personality. Vision, eventually, when everything else has been said and done, is about you and what you have realized, and continues to perceive. As a visionary, you need to establish your personality to your audience through your vision.

The audience that is looking for a challenging vision wants something that outflows the ordinary. They want something that they do not find in the pre-packaged, mass-produced and impersonal representation found in volume wholesale stores and other mass-appeal locations. This audience is looking for a vision that is original, real imaginations that demonstrates the personality of the visionary who created it.

This audience expects visionaries to be original and to express themselves through their work. In other words, this audience expects the work to be the expression of the visionary's personality. If this is not the case, if the work is impersonal, the visionary is perceived as being a lesser visionary. In other words, something is missing and this missing something is fundamental to vision.

Worse, if this is missing – i.e. the personality of the visionary demonstrated through his work- it will not be missing just from the work. It will also be missing from the way this leader talks about his vision. Some readers may find the above somewhat of an exaggeration. After all, some readers may believe that doing beautiful or interesting work is enough and that this work does not have to be about them and that it does not have to demonstrate their personality. This is a true statement, provided that your goal is not to express your vision, and eventually your personal style, in your work.

How can you express your vision and demonstrate your personal style unless you bring your personality into your work. As we saw, vision is by nature personal and personal style is not to be redundant. There is no way around it, unless you decide that expressing your vision and achieving a personal style is not something you want to do. If it is something you want to do then expressing your personality in your work is going to be necessary. You don't have to express all the aspects of your personality, in fact few artists do so, but you are going to have to express some aspects of your personality. The good thing is that you get to pick which aspects you want to show in your work, to some extent. A number of things can help you go through this thought-provoking effort. The first one is to remember your original birthplace, or sources, of inspiration.

II. CHAPTER TWO
A. WHAT A VISION IS

God's master plan

In God's master plan everyone is created with a vision. Though we might have many things in common with everyone else, yet each person is distinct from any other human being.
A vision begins as an idea in your imagination that you have a desire to make real. The idea turns into the intention and will to achieve that idea. Refining and clarifying the idea along with the intentions to achieve it are what turn into the vision.

The vision is the articulation of the desired future that is better in some important way than what exists or what is expected to exist in the future. First there is the mental creation and then the physical creation. We have to see it before we can shape it into reality. From a Christian perspective, vision is the ability to clearly see and articulate where God wants us to go or what God wants us to do in a given situation. Vision is the bridge between present and future reality. Vision is that magnet that attracts followers and resources.
Vision is the beginning point for leading the journey. It focuses and inspires, touches the heart and tightly focuses all of our sights and actions on that which we want to be tomorrow, not what we were yesterday or what we are today. The focus on vision disciplines us to think strategically. It is the framework for leading the journey.

Another definition for vision is, realistic, credible and attractive future for an organization.
Realistic: A vision must be based on reality to be meaningful for an organization.
Believable: A vision must be believable to be relevant. It must be credible to the employees or members of the organization. If the members of the organization do not find the vision credible, it will not be meaningful or serve a useful purpose. One of the purposes of a vision is to inspire those in the organization to achieve a level of excellence, and to provide purpose and direction for the work of those employees.

Striking: If a vision is going to inspire and motivate those in the organization, it must be attractive. People must want to be part of this future that's envisioned for the organization.

Future: A vision is not in the present, it is in the future. In this respect, the image of the leader gazing off into the distance to invent a vision may not be a bad one. A vision is not where you are now; it's where you want to be in the future.

The right vision for an organization, one that is realistic, believable, striking future, can accomplish a number of things for the organization:

It attracts commitment and energizes people. When people can see that the organization is committed to a vision-and that entails more than just having a vision statement-it generates enthusiasm about the course the organization intends to follow, and increases the commitment of people to work toward achieving that vision.

It creates meaning in workers' lives. A vision allows people to feel like they are part of a greater whole, and hence provides meaning for their work. The right vision will mean something to everyone in the organization if they can see how what they do contributes to that vision. Consider the difference between the driver who can only say, "I transport goods to and fro for the organization," to the one who can also say, "I am part of a team committed to becoming the worldwide leader in providing quality service to our customers." The work is the same, but the context and meaning of the work is different.

It establishes a standard of excellence

It serves a very important function in establishing a standard of excellence. In fact, a good vision is all about excellence. A vision so characterized by lack of excellence would not motivate or excite anyone about that organization.

The standard of excellence also can serve as a continuing goal and stimulate quality improvement programs, as well as providing a measure of the worth of the organization.

It bridges the present and the future. The right vision takes the organization out of the present, and focuses it on the future. It's easy to get caught up in the crises of the day, and to lose sight of where you were heading. A good vision can orient you on the future, and provide positive direction. The vision alone isn't enough to move you from the present to the future, however it is the desired future state for the organization; the strategic plan is how to get from where you are now to where you want to be in the future.

Kouzes and Posner describe the following four attributes of vision (The leadership challenge 1987, pp. 85-93):
Visions are future-oriented.
Visions describe the future in images or mental pictures.
Visions are about possibilities, not just probabilities.
Visions explain what is unique about the organization.
Vision should describe a set of ideas and priorities, a picture of the future, a sense of what makes the company special and unique, a core set of principles that the company stands for, and a broad set of compelling criteria that will help define organizational success."

Political and Corporate Vision

Political and Corporate vision is an inspiring proclamation of what the organization intends to become and to achieve at some point in the future. Vision refers to the category of intentions that are broad, all-inclusive and forward-thinking. It is the image that a business must have of its goals before it sets out to reach them. It describes aspirations for the future, without specifying the means that will be used to achieve those desired ends.
To choose a direction, an executive must have developed a mental image of the possible and desirable future state of the organization. This image, which we call a vision, may be as vague as a dream or as precise as a goal or a mission statement."

B. BENEFITS OF DEVELOPING A VISION

Vision is crucial to any organization. Any organization without vision is like a surgeon without a scalpel, a cowboy who has lost his horse, or a carpenter with a broken hammer. To attempt building an organization without a clear, well-articulated vision is to invite a stillbirth. Organizations and ministries may grow at the very beginning, but without a clear vision they are destined to plateau and eventually die. Here are few reasons:

Benefits of Vision Clarifies Direction

A characteristic of far too many North American ministries in general and organizations in particular is a lack of direction. They simply don't know where they are going, and many have not even thought about it. If they do not know where they are going- a lack of mission- then surely they cannot see where they are going- a lack of vision. The problem with not knowing or seeing where one is going is that you are liable to wind up just anywhere, and "just anywhere" will not do in today's world that is so desperately in need of direction.

A critical question that every organization must ask and revisit at least once a year is the directional question, where are we going? The answer is both the organization's mission and vision. The mission determines what the direction is; while the vision's particular concerns will be what the direction looks like. It is important that the visionary knows and sees the future of the organization.

Visionaries must be able to articulate what vision they have. Not to be able to do so is to invite disaster. When people follow a so-called leader who does not know where he is going, they all wind up in the common ditch. Also a leader cannot develop a plan to implement the organization without a clear target.

On numerous occasions, leaders in the Bible demonstrated leadership based on clear ministry direction. Moses demonstrated his acute knowledge of God's direction for the people of his generation when he appeared before Pharaoh and demanded their release (Exodus 5: 1-3). Afterward Moses and Aaron went in and told Pharaoh, "Thus saith the LORD God of Israel: "Let My people go, that they may hold a feast unto Me in the wilderness". And Pharaoh said, "Who is the LORD that I should obey his voice to let Israel go? I know not the LORD, neither will I let Israel go." And they said, "The God of the Hebrews hath met with us. Let us go, we pray thee, three days' journey into the desert and sacrifice unto the LORD our God, lest He fall upon us with pestilence or with the sword".

Nehemiah demonstrated that he knew precisely where he was going when he presented his vision to King Artaxerxes.

Nehemiah 2:5
^{5}And I said unto the king, "If it please the king, and if thy servant have found favor in thy sight, that thou wouldest send me unto Judah, unto the city of my fathers' sepulchers, that I may build it."
The people who are a part of the organization must know where it is going. People cannot

> *focus on fog. If God's people are to accomplish great things for him, they must know what it is they are setting out to accomplish.*

Most people who are a part of an organization fall into some problematic categories of direction. The largest category by far consists of organizations that have no vision and thus no idea where the organization is headed. Most of them are maintenance organizations that are headed nowhere. Neither the leaders nor the workers have any direction.

Another problematic category consists of organizations with multiple directions. These are organizations led by a leadership team in which each member has his or her own unique vision for the organization. One may envision a large member orientation for the organization. Another may envision a large productive and few workers orientation. While there is nothing wrong with any of the visions, an organization can sustain only a single vision. Most often an organization with multiple visions ends with a split. Actually the split was already cooking on the back burner from the very beginning of the organization; it only needed sufficient time to boil over and cause a major disaster.

Benefits of Vision Invites Unity

The first area of unity is in the recruitment of organization's personnel. A vision signals to all who desire to be a part of the organization precisely where that organization is going. It is a portrait of the organization's future. This gives potential participants an opportunity to both examine and determine their own personal vision in light of their gifts, passions, temperaments, talents, and abilities. The candidate is advanced if their personal vision closely matches the organization's direction, or whether they should look elsewhere for organization opportunities. In either case, keeping the vision in the forefront during recruitment protects continued organization cohesion. Job seekers will have a tip of problems before they are introduced into the organization.

The second area of unity is the retention of organization's personnel. Where there is a common vision, there will usually be harmony on the team. A good team consists of richly gifted people with diverse personalities who make significant but different contributions to the organization. That is why a wise leader will recruit staff members who have strong fits in areas where the leader is less gifted.

Vision functions as a cohesive factor; it holds the team together. The team consists of people who are creatively different, but a major reason they joined the team initially is because they passionately held to the same vision. Each person learns to appreciate and value the others, seeing how each one, though different, is necessary and contributes in a unique way to the accomplishment of their vision. They realize that they all need each other if anything significant is going to take place.

Vision is vital to another area, which is the retention of personnel. If regularly communicated, the vision serves as a constant reminder to those in the organization of the direction they have agreed to pursue together as a team. This is important because life is full of changes. People and organizations often change and adjust their direction. Clarity of the vision gives the people who make up the organization a chance to reevaluate the organization's direction in light of their own gifts and personal directions in life. But whether a person contemplates joining the organization or is already involved in that organization, a clear knowledge of direction best enhances organizational harmony.

Profits of Vision Accelerates Purpose

A characteristic of many organizations today is that they do not know what they are supposed to be doing. Others have strayed, having chosen maintenance over mission. If the typical business in the marketplace did not know what it was supposed to be doing or strayed, then it would not last a year before going out of business.

A question that every organization must regularly ask and revisit is the functional question; what are we supposed to be doing? Your vision as well as the mission answers this question. What the vision does uniquely for the organization is to paint a portrait of what it intends to accomplish so that all can see it. Vision communicates all these but does so pictorially. It provides people with a picture of what this process looks like. This is critical because if people cannot see it, then it probably will not happen.

Benefits of Vision Enhances Leadership

A question on the minds of many in an organization is where are the leaders? Organizations are facing a time in its history when many older leaders who have served well are reaching retirement age. The question thus becomes, who will replace them? The answer is today's generation and that of tomorrow. But what is essential to this new leadership? What will mark them and others as leaders? One answer is benefits of developing a vision into practicality. Developing a vision and then living it vigorously and authentically are essential elements of leadership. I define a leader as someone who knows and sees where he or she is going (mission and vision) and has followers (influence).

This definition has several characteristics. First, leaders are people who display character throughout the organization. They are people of integrity who exhibit fruit and produce trust. They are in the organization not because of what it can do for them but to serve others, and see where they are leading their organizations. They have a dynamic mission that enables them to know where they are going and, most important, a clear, energizing vision that helps them see that direction. Third, the result; a powerful, compelling vision is influence and it attracts and catalyzes followers (a good definition of leadership is influence). When an organization has a leader who owns a vision and powerfully lives that vision, they will follow that leader to the ends of the earth.

The long-term benefits are significant, however.

Vision:
- Breaks you out of limit thinking
- Provides continuity
- Identifies direction and purpose
- Alerts stakeholders to needed change
- Promotes interest and commitment
- Encourages openness to unique and creative solutions
- Encourages and builds confidence
- Builds loyalty through involvement (ownership)
- Results in efficiency and productivity
- The right vision attracts commitment and energizes people
- The right vision creates meaning in workers' and church members' lives
- The right vision establishes a standard of excellence
- The right vision bridges the present and the future

C. THE IMPORTANCE OF A VISION TO ANY LEADERSHIP, MINISTRY OR ORGANIZATION

Where there is no vision, the people perish" (Proverbs 29:18).

This is as true in business as it is in life.
Organizations whose leaders have no vision will suffer more frustration and wandering.
In August of 1964, under the backdrop of the Lincoln Memorial, Martin Luther King delivered the speech of his lifetime and perhaps the speech of his generation--a speech that served as the seedbed of social change. "I Have a Dream" was a **capsulated** summary of the dream that a generation of African Americans felt in their hearts. Dr. King was a leader. "I Have a Dream" was his vision.
What he saw was a better America--an America of equality and brotherhood. His dream has fueled a thousand other dreams and many of those dreams have become a reality. This is the power of vision. Every movement begins with a dream. The dream or vision is the force that invents and helps create the future.
Organizing for the long haul demands a sense of vision, a sense of where we are going. If we only see the short-term tasks before us, it is easy to become frustrated and discouraged. Everyone needs a sense of the vision. We must be constantly reminded of our short-term and our long-term goals. We must review how our work contributes toward meeting both sets of goals.
Vision, like self-confidence, isn't achieved by taking a pill or reading a book. A sense of vision grows out of a set of values, experiences, individual reflections, and organizational wisdom and direction. If we see how our work supports and contributes to the larger vision, our work will seem more meaningful and can be more directed. For leaders, a vision is not a dream; it is a reality that has yet to come into existence. It gives a leader purpose, and the power of the vision and the leader's devotion to it work to inspire others.
Warren Bennis, having spent many years working with leaders, has concluded: (Bennis 1990)
Peter Kreeft, a professor of philosophy at Boston College, says that "to be a leader you have to lead people to a goal worth having--something that's really good and really there" (Stewart 1991). That essential "something" is the vision. A Vision Prompts Passion.

One of the problems that leaders face in their organizations - especially in today's smaller, struggling organizations - is the mediocrity problem. They are not giving enough attention to what they do and how they do it. Far too often, for example, office duties tend to be poorly planned and poorly executed.

Over a period of years, organizations can allow itself to lapse into a maintenance mentality- it just seems to be getting by- that over time leads to mediocrity. Every day is business as usual. The people come to the office but often seem to be going through the motions. When they leave, not much has happened to them and not a lot takes place in their lives during the week. The younger generations will not tolerate this for long before they leave and look for a better place to work.

Vision and passion work hand in hand. While vision is a seeing what involves what leaders see in their heads, passion is a feeling that involves their emotions- what they feel in their hearts. Passionate people are those who feel strongly about "something". The "something" in this context is the vision. A compelling, clear vision fuels passion. When leaders get a vision they see what their organization could be, something marvelous happens. That vision most often results in an energetic, infectious sense of passion. People can feel it as well, catch the vision and experience this passion, and then the organization can re-create itself to become more effective in mission.

A Vision Fosters Risk Taking

A shared vision fosters risk taking by an organization's members. When the visionary casts the vision, everyone knows what needs to be done, we can see it in our head. The question that needs to be answered by the visionary is how will we accomplish it? The people who believe in the visionary are willing to take risk for the vision.

Five important things that a well-articulated vision accomplishes

- Recruitment - vision encourages volunteers and resources. Movements with clear vision are much more likely to grow and attract visionary workers than those that simply copy someone else's program. Like-minded people ask for the opportunity to be involved. Donors ask how they can help.

- Retention - vision gets and keeps people on board and tries to retain them.
- Direction - vision constantly reminds us of the direction we've agreed to pursue.
- Re-evaluates - vision continues to evaluate the organization's direction in light of the vision.
- Relevance - vision focuses on the cutting edge of effectiveness.

III. CHAPTER THREE
A. THE PROCESS OF DEVELOPING A VISION

The process of visioning comes first before strategic planning. Consider these points and be sure to:
- Draw on the beliefs, mission, and environment of the organization
- Describe what you want to see in the future
- Be specific to each organization
- Be positive and inspiring
- Be open to dramatic modifications to current organization, methodology, teaching techniques, facilities, etc.

Thinking Through Your Purpose

When you are thinking through your purpose, consider these three questions
- What is your purpose?
- What is your value?
- What is your believe?

Key Components for Your Vision

Incorporate your beliefs in your vision
Your beliefs must meet your organizational goals as well as community goals
Your beliefs are a statement of your values
Your beliefs are a public & visible declaration of your expected outcomes
Your beliefs must be precise and practical
Your beliefs will guide the actions of all involved
Your beliefs reflect the knowledge, philosophy, and actions of all
Your beliefs are a key component of strategic planning

B. MAKING YOUR VISION REALITY

Having a vision for the future can be a source of inspiration; it provides clear decision-making criteria. One needs to know where you are, your current resources, your current obstacles, and where you want to go - the vision for the future.

It's amazing what one can achieve from having a clear vision and the determination to make it a reality.
One needs to stick with a vision step-by-step, and inspire like-minded people to get involved. At times it will be a slow process, but continue to get over every obstacle in the path. The chosen path may be difficult, but with determination, it shall come to pass! When working toward a goal, all the answers are not needed to start. All that is needed to know is what the next step is, and hold a willingness to trust that everything will work out.
Start stretching your concept of what is possible for your life.
Right now there probably is a mental set point of achievement that is opened. In reality, your set point might be much higher than you think! Begin expanding on your dreams and see what else you can do to grow and develop your potential.

Networking with others

Networking with other people can help you move mountains. It's an amazing achievement when you finally realize your vision. Not just for you but for everyone who has shared the vision.
Put your heart and soul into achieving it. As you start your journey with belief, you will find positive ways of making your dreams a reality. Your enthusiasm will shine through and is likely to inspire others who will help you on your way.
    Make a plan to inspire like-minded people to get involved. Also, make it a point to get to know like-minded friends who are on the same journey as you. Just think about the joy when you finally realize your vision and being able to share with everyone with the same vision.
Internalize your vision by writing it down and putting this piece of paper where you can clearly see it every day. Then set about writing down your daily, monthly or yearly goals in order to achieve this vision.
At times, you may feel daunted by your lack of progress or feel disheartened by the obstacles that are thrown in your path. Hence it is important that you do not lose sight of your vision. If others can succeed in spite of all difficulties, so can you.
    You may not have the answers on how to get there. But you can start by making a commitment to your vision and take a step each day towards it. Have the trust that everything will work out.

Start opening up your mind to the possibilities of what may be possible. To accomplish great things, we must not only act, but also dream; not only plan, but also believe.

Creating a vision requires careful thought, personal insights, and engaging the mind for answers. When a decision is reached on a vision that inspires, go for it with all your heart and soul. As you start your journey with belief, opportunities will come along to help make your dreams a reality.

C. THE LEADER'S ROLE IN BIRTHING THE VISION

Cultivating and creating the vision by the visionary

Much of the process of developing the vision falls on the shoulders of the primary vision caster. I charge leaders with these three responsibilities:
- Establish clear direction
- Communicate the vision and secure commitment to move ahead
- Energize, motivate and inspire people to overcome the obstacles that will surely arise

The team leader must begin the process. Take time to think, read, study, listen, ask questions, pray and reflect. Vision is the product of learning from the past, correctly assessing the present and seeing how the future could be different and better. Sometimes vision is the fruit of months of thinking and reflection. At other times it is that flash of brilliance that is right for the situation. Vision often arises from an unmet need or untapped opportunity.

Ask yourself, "What am I really dissatisfied with?" "What needs to be done that is not being done?" "What are we uniquely positioned and equipped to do?" "What untapped opportunities lie before us?" "What is God doing around us?" "What are my dissatisfactions, desires, hopes and dreams for the future?"

Look over other vision statements from churches, other organizations and movements, or businesses.

Make it worthwhile. Daniel Burnam, the chief architect who rebuilt Chicago after the fire is credited with saying,

"Make no small plans for they have no ability to stir men's blood." Think of the scope of the vision that Jesus cast--"Preach the gospel to all the nations," "Make disciples of all the nations."

To ask God for a God-sized vision fits well within the parameters of Ephesians 3:20--"

> *Now to him who is able to do immeasurably more than all we ask or imagine...*"

Begin recording your vision in a 3-ring binder with dividers sectioned off into the specifics elements of the vision to be developed. This simple tool allows the vision to be recorded and modified. The first draft is almost always formulated by the primary vision caster. Make up a binder for all who will eventually help shape the vision. The notebook should include:
- Purpose
- Mission
- Vision
- Values and guiding principles
- Position
- Target audience
- Strategic imperatives
- Core competencies
- Key objectives

Challenge the vision. Step away from it and let it roast for a while. Is it clear, energizing, visual, future oriented, culturally relevant, realistic yet challenging, etc.?

Revise and modify the vision with your team--those who are responsible for its implementation. The process takes time, is cluttered and difficult but is as necessary as the product itself.

The Visionary

The visionary or leader (Founder) is the sole point person or primary leader of the organization. This person can be known as the Apostle, Senior Pastor, or in the Para church the President (Religious Organizations) Chief Executive Officer, General Director and so on. It is important to recognize that every organization and every leadership team within an organization needs a single leader. From a practical perspective all the participants in an organization or on a leadership team are not identical in their leadership abilities, knowledge, experience, reputation, training, and commitment. Some are born with natural gifts of leadership and others have been blessed and gifted in other areas for the organization.

It takes a visionary leader to cultivate a profound, positive vision of the future. For example
Visionary leaders must begin to do the vision and people will follow.
They must expose themselves regularly to as many sources of information as possible.
They must read lots of books and articles on leadership change and so on.
They must listen to tapes on the same and attend selected conferences put on by the various visionaries from different churches and organizations.

If possible the visionary must pursue a yearlong, full-time internship in an organization that shares a similar vision and is prospering. The experience gained from such an internship would be invaluable. All of these sources will supply the visionary leader with a constant flow of raw data for the mind to digest. It takes work to do the vision – go and knock on doors to bring it to past. The visionary wears three hats:

1. Cultivator
2. Communicator
3. Clarifier of the vision

Vision cultivator

The vision cultivator initiates and develops the organization's unique vision, which empowers the vision community for the organization. He initiates the process by challenging the organization to come up with a clear, challenging vision. He develops the vision initially but solicits the input of others to the extent that it becomes everyone's vision.

Vision Communicator

The visionary is the message, he functions as the primary vision caster though not the only vision caster. Once the vision is cultivated and in place, the leader must take responsibility to keep it before the organization & community. He does this directly and indirectly through others in the organization. Without the regular casting and recasting of the dream, people in the community are quick to stop dreaming and often behave as if there is no vision at all.

The visionary must always have these four things:
1. *Be prepared:* it is essential because whenever you speak to people, they believe you know your subject more than them and are ready prepared.
2. *Make others comfortable:* you have to be comfortable and excited to share your vision to people so that they can also be comfortable and excited in listening. Share how the vision has been applied to your life.
3. *Be committed:* Facial expression, body language, eye contact, simplicity, clarity, posture, and audibility is very important when communicating the vision. Make sure you believe in what you are talking about.
4. *Be interesting:* - think creatively, historical, what is familiar to your audience. Give illustration, connect, personal testimony, familiar sayings, life experiences, give a list and people love to write. Incorporate different expressions with vivid pictures. Make them emotional, poetic, expressive descriptive impact, conditions, references, flowing words (not amazement words), old philosophical sayings, etc.

Vision clarifier

Finally, the vision clarifier focuses on the vision. Cutting edge organizations are characterized by a whirlwind of activity and catastrophic change. In the midst of all these, there must be someone who regularly serves to rethink and further refine the dream. He helps people comprehend the vision and discover their part in it. He supplies precision answers as to how, when, and where those in the vision community can play a significant role in the realization of the dream.

This clarification means periodic revisiting and rephrasing of the vision. The clarifier is not changing the vision but looking for new, creative ways to express it as a means of infusing fresh life and power into the dream.

Clarification helps to determine if it is time to rethink and possibly change the dream. Fred Smith argues that the mark of a good leader is to "know" when it is time to change the vision. "he gives as an indicator, the demographic changes that can take place in the community and in the organization. Other indicators might be a change in leadership and or the purpose of the organization.

IV. CHAPTER FOUR
A. IMPLEMENTATION OF THE VISION

Without the full commitment of the organization's senior executives, it is hard to start strategic planning. Participants will feel fooled and misled. A vision statement and a mission statement, along with this year's goals, filed, unimplemented in a cabinet or computer is a serious source of negativity and poor employee morale.

Leaders can do the following to create a successful strategic planning process:

- Establish a clear vision for the strategic planning process.
- Paint a picture of where the organization will end up and the anticipated outcomes.
- Make certain the picture is one of reality and not what people "wish" would occur.
- Make sure key employees know "why" the organization has such a vision.
- Appoint an executive champion or leader who "owns" the strategic planning process. Make certain other senior managers, as well as other appropriate people in the organization involve. Executive support in strategic planning is critical to its success. Executives must lead, support, follow-up, and live the results of the strategic planning process. These are additional ways executive leaders can support the strategic planning process.
- Establish a structure which will support the move to a more strategically thinking and acting organization. This may take the form of a Steering Committee, Leadership Group, Core Planning Team or Guiding Coalition.
- Change the measurement systems, reward, and recognition systems. Measure and reward the accomplishment of the new expectations established through the strategic planning process. Develop within to communicate, reinforce, and provide a structure that supports the accomplishment of the strategic planning goals.

While every person in your organization cannot make their voice heard on every issue within the strategic planning, you must solicit and act upon feedback from other members of the organization. Integral in the strategic planning process must be the commitment of each executive to discuss the process and the plans with staff members. Too often, executives hold information closely and consolidate their own dysfunctional power within the organization at the expense of other company employees feeling - and acting - excluded.

Throughout the strategic planning process, treat people with the same respect you expect from them. With your vision statement, mission statement, values, strategies, goals, and action plans developed and shared, it will be a win, both personally and professionally.

Consider these few points:

Step 1 – Increase urgency.
Leaders use compelling visions that others can touch, see and feel. Look for ways to reduce complacency and identify compelling opportunities. People start telling each other about the vision when they feel the urgency.

Step 2 – Build the guiding team.
A group powerful enough to guide a big change is formed and they start to work together well. The group consists of powerful change agents including those who know enough about the vision of the organization. Those who can do something about it and those who care enough to get the job done, must be selected.

Step 3 – Get the vision right.
The guiding team develops the right strategy. They develop compelling possibility that responds to the heart as well as the head. They link bold visions to bold strategies and find ways of involving others in the visioning process.

Step 4 - Communicate for buy-in.
People begin to buy into the vision, and this shows in their behavior. Communications are simple, heart-felt and appeal to people's emotions. Visionary behaviors are modeled especially by leaders.

Step 5 – Empower action.
More people feel able to act, and do act, on the vision. Customers are rewarded and supported and are used to influence skeptics. Barriers to progress are identified and gradually removed. People receive feedback which helps them to relate better to the vision.

Step 6 – Create short term wins.
Wins which touch the emotions come thick and fast. Successes speak to influential players who may not be fully engaged. Momentum builds as people try to fulfill the vision, while fewer and fewer resist change.

Step 7 – Don't let up.

People make wave after wave of changes until the vision is fulfilled. Urgency and support are maintained. Distractions are reduced. Opportunities and resources supporting the vision are taken up.
Step 8 – Make change stick.

Implementing a Vision

How is idea of an organization turned into implementation? First recruit people to the vision and develop leaders to take portions of the organization. Let people know how they can be involved when you go out. Print a simple material to take with you.

Volunteers:

Network at public notices, laundry mates, stores, newspaper, local colleges, local churches, etc. Tell them your organization is offering training. Ask people on personal basis & borrow people from different churches to start your own until yours is growing. Recruit group leaders and finance teams. In recruitment, let people know what is available, time and work. Equip the people that you recruit by perfecting and preparing them.

B. SHARED VISION

Sharing the vision with others

Creating a vision is one thing, passing it on to others is quite another. Vision sharing involves a sender, a message and a receiver. The sender initially is the leader. Who you are as a leader and a person is of utmost significance. The credibility of the messenger influences the message.

Aligning with the vision is to align oneself with the vision caster. The credibility of the vision caster primarily is based on the perceptions of the leader's track record, his character, his personal commitment to the vision and the credibility of the vision itself. Also remember that if you are married, the first person to share in your vision is your wife.

An important aspect of vision is the notion of "shared vision." "Some studies indicate that it is the presence of this personal vision on the part of a leader. This is shared with members of the organization that may differentiate true leaders from mere managers" (Manasse, 1986, p. 151, italics added).

A leader's vision needs to be shared by those who will be involved in the realization of the vision. Murphy (1988). When applied shared vision to previous studies of policy makers and policy implementation; he found that those studies identified gaps between policy development and its implementation and concluded that this gap also applies to current discussions of vision. He stressed the need for the development of a shared vision. "It is rare to see a clearly defined vision articulated by a leader at the top of the hierarchy and then installed by followers" (Murphy, 1988, p. 656). Whether the vision of an organization is developed collaboratively or initiated by the leader and agreed to by the followers, it becomes the common ground, the shared vision that compels all involved. "Vision comes alive only when it is shared" (Westley & Mintzberg, 1989, p. 21).
Young Joshua and Caleb did a great job of casting the vision in Numbers 13 but lacked the credibility of experience to align the Israelites with the vision of entering the Promised Land. The vision was cast but not caught. Imparting the vision is too important to be left to chance.

To effectively cast the vision you must:
- Be personally committed to fulfilling the vision
- Know your audience. You must know how fulfilling the vision will benefit or affect your audience.

Use example, metaphor and analogy. Use story telling more than statistics. Engage the hearts and minds of your audience. Speak positively. Use multiple forums (big meetings, small groups, formal and informal interaction) and repetition.
It should be written down, published, posted and frequently talked about.

> *Habakkuk 2:2*
> *And the LORD answered me and said: "Write the vision and make it plain upon tablets, that he may run that readeth it".*

Meet with each department leader or leadership team and walk him or her through the process. Help them to catch the vision by helping them see their department in light of the vision. This is vital in recruiting others to the vision. The primary tool you have in recruitment is the vision itself. It is "the magnet that attracts." Begin with those who are most influential and will most likely be aligned with you and the vision. Don't be surprised that people come on board at different rates. Some may never be aligned.

Listen and welcome feedback. Make revisions as you progress so that although it is a singular vision it has many fingerprints on it.

Both catching the vision and casting the vision is ultimately very important. To catch the vision is to be associated with the vision. Without alignment to the vision you will not be able to move in the same direction and have the motivation to keep moving ahead through the obstacles. This act of alignment is the critical step between vision casting and implementation.

To bring about significant change requires a team to own the dream. To introduce a plan before aligning your team is to insure a slow, frustrating death of the vision. People who disagree with the "ends" will argue about every "means." In the process of support from your team you are really building the foundations of team commitment, cooperation and community.

How do you know when people have caught the vision? The simplest test is this: those who catch the vision are able to cast the vision. They have moved from customer to salesman of the vision. They are actively involved in recruiting others. It is the freshly recruited Andrew inviting his brother Peter to join with them.

C. SOME GREAT VISIONARIES

Every now and then God calls a man to a task so big that few can equal the challenge. Above all else, these leaders are visionaries.

Visionaries are the builders of a new dawn, working with imagination, insight, and boldness. They present a challenge that calls forth the best in people and brings them together around a shared sense of purpose. They work with the power of intentionality and alignment with a higher purpose. Their eyes are on the horizon, not just on the near at hand. They are social innovators and change agents, seeing the big picture and thinking strategically.

There is a deep interconnectedness between the visionaries and the whole. True visionary leaders serve the good of the whole. They search for solutions that go beyond the usual adversarial approaches and address the fundamental level of problems. They find a higher combination of the best of both sides of an issue and address the root causes of problems to create real breakthroughs.

Great visionaries have

- *Vision* - More than anything else, great leaders are driven by great dreams. They're pulled along by the grip of providence. Invariably, the force of their personalities pulls us along with them.
- *Innovation* - Great leaders give the world "ideas" that change the existing order. They convey creativity and imagination. They embrace an uncertain future.
- *Sacrifice* - Great leaders deny themselves for a greater good. They're so committed to their cause that they are willing to risk rejection.
- *Integrity* - At their central part great leaders have steadfast character. A handshake still means everything to them. This inspires confidence.
- *Optimism* - Great leaders possess a passion that touches that noble desire in each of us. They inspire us to want to be part of something bigger than ourselves.
- *Never Give Up* - Great leaders display unwavering belief in their mission. Against all odds they show persistence, perseverance, and faithfulness to their call. Their motivation rests on deeply held principles, not opinion polls.
- *Ability* - Great visionaries possess special abilities. They are people of skill, whether inventor, philosopher, theologian, scientist, artist, writer, poet, or preacher. They possess natural intelligence.
- *Relate to others* - Great visionaries have understanding and love for people. Their people skills include compassion, and listening. They relate to people from all walks of life.
- *Impossibility* - Great visionaries never think they are possible. They are marked by a profound humility. The world would not pick them. And if in their own lifetimes they become great, they are the last ones to know.

- ***Excellence*** - Great visionaries demand excellence from themselves, which urges us to be like them. Their motivation for excellence is often confused with perfectionism.
- ***Servant of Others*** - Great visionaries are first servant leaders. Great leaders do what they do to bring life changing experience to people. They exist to serve humanity by first denying who they are so they can serve others.

V. CHAPTER FIVE
A. VISION STATEMENT

Developing Effective Vision and Mission Statements

The Procedure for Writing a Vision Statement

Malphurs (1997) breaks down the procedure for developing a vision statement into three components: personnel, process, and product. With respect to personnel, he strongly recommends that the founder of the organization, political leader or the senior pastor ("the point person of the organization or the ministry team") should have primary responsibility for developing the vision statement.

Herrington, Bonem, and Furr (2000) also recommend that the CEO, leader, political leader or senior pastor develop the draft of the vision statement. The senior pastor is best qualified to do this because of his education, experience, and giftedness. If he is not qualified to do this, then why did the church hire him in the first place?

Malphurs describes the role of the other ministry leaders in three terms: cooperation, support, and communication. Barna (1992) also emphasizes the primary role of the senior pastor to the exclusion of others in the process.

Dale (1986) also promotes opening up the process to greater participation by using a "town-meeting" approach. He also envisions a process where draft statements are presented to the leadership team and to the congregation for feedback and revision.

A vision statement provides many of the same benefits as the mission statement, but it also includes other benefits. Nanus says that a vision statement can unleash the following four forces in an organization (1992, pp. 16-17):

Fortune 500 Company has its mission posted in every cubicle: "To continuously exceed our customers' increasing expectations." It sounds ambitious, but raises a lot more questions as well. Who are these customers? What expectations do they have? How can one contribute to fulfilling this mission? And how long did it take a group of highly paid executives to choose that particular mission statement over "To be the number one company in the industry" or "To be recognized as a worldwide leader in excellence"?

When used properly, vision and mission statements can be very powerful tools, especially for new and small firms. Just as a successful coach has a vision for putting a team together and game plans for successful execution, vision and mission provide direction for a new or small firm, without which it is difficult to develop a cohesive plan. In turn, this allows the firm to pursue activities that lead the organization forward and avoid devoting resources to activities that do not.

Vision statements and mission statements are very different. A vision statement for a new or small firm spells out goals at a high level and should coincide with the founder's goals for the business. Simply put, the vision should state what the founder ultimately envisions the business to be, in terms of growth, values, employees, contributions to society, and the like. Therefore, self-reflection by the founder is a vital activity if a meaningful vision is to be developed. As a founder, once you have defined your vision, you can begin to develop strategies for moving the organization toward that vision. Part of this includes the development of a company mission. A good vision statement will have the ring of authenticity and carries with it a sense of "sensation!"

To be effective it must be:
- Relevant
- Motivating
- Memorable.

Vision statements that fall short usually have at least one of these elements missing. President Kennedy's vision in April 1961 to "put a man on the moon by the end of the decade," though short, was a clear and compelling image of what could be and should be. Here are a few sample vision statements to be considered:
"Win the marketplace today, win the world tomorrow"
"Winning a corporation to reach a nation," "Building a spiritual legacy"
"Year after year, Westin and its people will be regarded as the best and most sought after hotel and resort management group in North America." (Westin Hotels)
"To be recognized and respected as one of the premier associations of HR Professionals." (HR Association of Greater Detroit)
"Building a community to reach a community"
"Putting the gospel within arm's reach of every person on the planet,"
"Whatever it takes--wherever it takes us," etc.

A Vision statement can paint a picture that creates a sense of desire and builds commitment to reaching the vision. It is seeing what is possible. A vision statement is about the impact to be made on the world; it defines a long-term dream.

Malphurs offers seven purposes that a vision statement can accomplish (1999, pp. 134-7):
1. Encourages unity
2. Creates energy
3. Provides purpose
4. Fosters risk taking.
5. Enhances leadership
6. Promotes excellence
7. Sustains ministry

Differences between a Mission Statement and Vision Statement

The vision statement should be carefully distinguished from the mission statement. One difference noted by Nanus (1992) is that the mission statement describes the purpose of the organization and the vision statement describes the direction. Barna states that, "while the mission statement is philosophic in nature, the vision statement is strategic in character" (1992, p. 39).

Here are some additional distinctions. The mission statement is formulated as one sentence, and it may apply equally as well to a number of organizations. The vision statement, however, may be a paragraph, a page, or a multipage document that describes how this particular organization will fulfill that mission in its particular context. Consequently, the vision statement will apply only to the particular organization that wrote it. But an organization does not share its vision with any other organization. If another organization is fulfilling the same vision, then why do both need to exist?

1. The mission statement is a statement; the vision statement is a picture or snapshot.
2. The mission statement is applied primarily in strategic planning; the vision statement is applied primarily in communication of the leaders to the people.

3. The vision statement is longer than the mission statement.
4. The purpose of a mission statement is to inform people; the purpose of a vision statement is to inspire people.
5. The mission statement results in doing; the vision statement results in seeing.
6. The source of the mission statement is the head; the source of the vision statement is the heart.
7. The mission statement is developed first; the vision statement then expands upon it.
8. The mission may be common to a number of organizations; the vision is unique to one organization.
9. The mission statement has a broad focus; the vision statement has a narrow focus.
10. The effect of the mission statement is clarity; the effect of the vision statement is challenge.
11. Development of a mission statement is a science that can be taught; development of a vision statement is an art that must be caught.
12. The mission statement is best communicated visually; the vision statement is best communicated verbally.

A mission statement provides the action needed to reinforce a Vision Statement. A mission is what you intend to accomplish. A well-written mission statement demonstrates that you understand your business, have defined your unique focus, and can articulate your objectives concisely to yourself and others. A vision is a statement about what your organization wants to become. It should resonate with all members of the organization and help them feel proud, excited, and part of something much bigger than themselves. A vision should stretch the organization's capabilities and image of itself. It gives shape and direction to the organization's future. Visions range in length from a couple of words to several pages.

B. MISSION STATEMENT

- Purpose
- Priorities
- Expression of vision

Mission Statements for New and Small Firms

The mission statement should be a concise statement of business strategy and developed from the customer's perspective. It should fit with the vision for the business. The mission should answer three questions:
- What do we do?
- How do we do it?
- For whom do we do it?

What do we do? This question should not be answered in terms of what is physically delivered to customers, but by the real and/or psychological needs that are fulfilled when customers buy your products or services. Customers make purchase decisions for many reasons. It includes economical, logistical, and emotional factors. An excellent illustration of this is a business in the Twin Cities that imports hand-made jewelry from East Africa. When asked what her business does, the owner replied, "We import and market east African jewelry." But when asked why customers buy her jewelry, she explained that, "They're buying a story in where the jewelry came from." This is an important distinction and answering this question from the need-fulfilled perspective will help you answer the other two questions effectively.

How do we do it? This question captures the more technical elements of the business. Your answer should encompass the physical product or service. It should emphasize how it is sold and delivered to customers and it should fit with the need that the customer fulfills with its purchase. In the example above, the business owner had originally defined her business as selling East African jewelry and was attempting to sell it on shelves of boutique retail stores with little success. After modifying the answer to the first question, she realized that she needed to deliver the story to her customers along with the product. She began organizing wine parties that included a slide show of East Africa. Stories of personal experiences there, and pictures and descriptions of the villagers who make the jewelry was known. This method of delivery has been very successful for her business.

For whom do we do it? The answer to this question is also vital; as it will help you focus your marketing efforts. Though many small business owners would like to believe otherwise, not everyone is a potential customer. Customers will almost always have both demographic and geographic limitations. When starting out, it is generally a good idea to define the demographic characteristics (age, income, etc.) of customers who are likely to buy. Then, define a geographic area in which your business can gain a presence. As you grow, you can add new customer groups and expand your geographic focus.

An additional consideration with mission statements is that most businesses will have multiple customer groups that purchase for different reasons. In these cases, one mission statement can be written to answer each of the three questions for each customer group or multiple mission statements can be developed. Also, as a final thought, remember that your vision and mission statements are meant to help guide the business, not to lock you into a particular direction. As your company grows and as the competitive environment changes, your mission may require change to include additional or different needs fulfilled, delivery systems, or customer groups. With this in mind, your vision and mission should be revisited periodically to determine whether modifications are desirable.

Peter Drucker writes: *"What matters is not the leader's charisma. What matters is the leader's mission.* Therefore, the first job of the leader is to think through and define the mission of the institution." I am convinced that a dynamic organization's mission is as important as a clear, challenging vision.
Indeed, the act of leadership is fundamentally the act of articulating first a mission statement and then pursuing it.

Mission Statement

Mission is a precise description of what an organization does. It should describe the business the organization is in. It is a definition of "why" the organization exists currently. Each member of an organization should be able to verbally express this mission.
Additionally, each person needs a mission for his or her life. The alignment of your life mission with your organization's mission is one of the key factors in whether you are happy with your work and workplace. If they are incongruent, you are likely dissatisfied with your work choice.

Mission Statement Samples
"Our goal is simply stated. We want to be the best service organization in the world." (IBM) "FedEx is committed to our People-Service-Profit

Philosophy. We will produce outstanding financial returns by providing totally reliable, competitively superior, global, air-ground transportation of high-priority goods and documents that require rapid, time-certain delivery." (Federal Express)

"To give ordinary folk the chance to buy the same thing as rich people." (Wal-Mart)

"Our mission is to earn the loyalty of Saturn owners and grow our family by developing and marketing U.S.-manufactured vehicles that are world leaders in quality, cost, and customer enthusiasm through the integration of people, technology, and business systems." (Saturn)

"In order to realize our Vision, our Mission must be to exceed the expectations of our customers, whom we define as guests, partners, and fellow employees. (Mission) We will accomplish this by committing to our shared values and by achieving the highest levels of customer satisfaction, with extraordinary emphasis on the creation of value. (Strategy) In this way we will ensure that our profit, quality and growth goals are met." (Westin Hotels and Resorts)

The most important time to design and develop a dynamic mission statement is at the very beginning of your organization.

C. CORE VALUES

Core Values are rather simple; they outline the ethics and values of the company, creating a pledge to its clients and the world at large. These statements demonstrate a company's commitment to success. A commitment to values is an outstanding characteristic of all visionary leaders. They embody a sense of personal integrity, and radiate a sense of energy, vitality and will. Will is a spiritual attribute, which allows a leader to stand for something.

More self-aware and reflective than others, visionary leaders follow an inner sense of direction, and lead from the inside out, as exemplified by Mahatma Gandhi. He said, "I must first be the change I want to see in my world." He was a prime example of a commitment to values, as he freed India by appealing to the moral conscience of Britain and using "satyagraha" or non-violent action to reveal the immorality of the British Empire.

Rather than being corrupted by power, visionary leaders are elevated by power and exercise moral leadership. Mary Robinson, former President of Ireland and U.N. High Commissioner for Human Rights, embodies this type of moral leadership, Kofi Annan from Ghana W/A, former president of the United Nations for ten years has ruled with dignity and core values of helping mankind, as does Marion Wright Edelman, founder of the Children's Defense Fund, who has a deep commitment to children's welfare.

Many successful leaders in business, such as Jeffrey Swartz of Timberland Shoes, have demonstrated the power of living their values. Swartz pays employees to volunteer in the community and honors the "double bottom line"-profit and values". Tom Chappell, CEO of Tom's of Maine, found that he could "do well by doing good." Doing good-- embodying his values--has made his company very profitable. Tom's of Maine uses all natural ingredients in their products to protect consumers and the environment.

VI. CHAPTER SIX
A. COMMUNICATING YOUR VISION

Communications:

Confidently build internal communications from senior management to your employees, assuring them of their value to your organization. You cannot over-communicate when you are asking your organization to change. Every successful executive, who has led a change management effort, in my experience, makes this statement. Communication is one of the toughest issues in organizations.

Communicate Your Company Identity: Your company identity includes
Business name
Logo
Tagline
Vision, Mission, Core Values
Company colors
Graphics other than logos

Communication Materials:
Letterhead (also a marketing material)
Envelopes
Fax cover sheets
Invoices
E-mail signature (also a marketing material)

Marketing Materials:
Letterhead
E-mail signature
Business cards
Sales letters
Brochures
Flyers
Newsletters, etc.

How to choose a company Name: Choosing a company name is one of the most exciting parts of starting a business. It adds a sense of reality to the process. A successful business name must contain two components.
Descriptive component tells your clients what it is you do. You want to ensure that your market does not have to guess at what you do.
Distinctive component is what sets your company apart from everyone else in your industry.

A good business name accomplishes a number of goals.

It is direct. You do not want anything in your business name that could potentially confuse a potential client about what it is you do.
It is not trendy. Stay away from names identified to current trends. Trends come and go.
It conveys a right feeling. You want to choose a name that triggers a positive association.
It is easy to spell and pronounce. Make it simple; a name which is easily spelled is easily remembered. People have a hard time remembering names they cannot pronounce.
It is memorable. It is hard enough choosing a name, not to mention one that is memorable. Of course this is not always possible.
It is pleasing to the ear. Whether something is pleasing or not has a lot to do with your market. Once you have list of prospective names share with family, friends & colleagues.

Company Logo:
The word ''logo'' means a name, symbols or trademark designed for easy recognition. A good logo will convey something about your company, even a feeling.
A logo is an image that is associated with your company and gives the public another way to remember you. Your logo appears on all of your correspondence, business cards, letterhead, flyers and advertisements. The purpose of a logo is to convey the essence of your company's identity. When thinking of your logo design, consider these items; graphics, typestyle, and tagline and make an effort to notice other company logos, especially within the VA profession.
Logo Color is an important element. Bright colors will attract attention and excite people; blues and grays have a conservative theme.

A Tagline is one of the most important ways to market your business; it can become the basis of your advertising and marketing pieces. Tag lines do not have to be "catchy" but they should be memorable to your target audience. A general rule is the shorter the better.

Branding is a name, term, design, symbol, feature or identity which distinguishes your service from others. Strong brands can deliver incredible customer loyalty, and your service could become synonymous with price, quality or some other feature.

A good brand will contain three elements otherwise known as the three "Cs".

- *Clarity:* strong brands immediately tell you what they do and do not stand for.
- *Consistency:* for effective brand, surrounding message must be consistent over time.
- *Constancy:* strong brands are constantly in front of their target audiences.

Visual Aids:

You can create word pictures in your audience's mind, drawing them into the scene that you describe, and thereby gain or keep their attention focused on your ideas. Martin Luther King Jr. was an astute student of visualization in creating such word pictures, especially in " I Have a Dream" speech. Winston Churchill was another wordsmith whose use of language gave courage to a nation in a perilous hour. This particular strategy is one that can be used in combination with others; in fact, most of the strategies we have discussed are capable of being used alone or in combination.

The function of visual aids:

To enhance understanding of the topic
To add authenticity
To help your speech have lasting impact
To enhance speaker ethos

B. GREAT LEADERS COMMUNICATE THEIR VISION

A visionary may dream wonderful visions of the future and articulate them with great inspiration. A visionary is good with words. But a visionary leader is good with actions as well as words, and so can bring his/her vision into being in the world, thus transforming it in some way. More than words are needed for a vision to take form in today's world. It requires the total package of communication, leadership and heartfelt commitment.

A visionary leader is effective in manifesting his or her vision because he or she communicates specific, achievable goals, initiates action and enlists the participation of others.

The mysterious inner process within leaders that enables them to work their supernatural and radiate the charisma that mobilizes others for a higher purpose is good communication of the vision.

Visionary leadership is based on a balanced expression of the spiritual, mental, emotional and physical dimensions. It requires core values, clear vision, empowering relationships, and innovative action. When one or more of these dimensions are missing, leadership cannot manifest a vision.

A Clear, Communicative, Inspirational Vision

Visionaries who are successful at manifesting their visions base their leadership on an inspirational, positive picture of the future, as well as a clear sense of direction as to how to get there. Vision is a field that brings energy into form. Effective leaders broadcast a consistent message by themselves embodying their vision. They keep communicating the vision to create a strong field which then brings their vision into physical reality. Nelson Mandela clearly held a positive vision of a racially harmonious South Africa during his 28 years in jail and helped bring it into reality peacefully, to the amazement of the world.

The best visionary leaders move energy to a higher level by offering a clear vision of what is possible through communication. They inspire people to be better than they already are and help them identify with what God has created in them." This was the power of Martin Luther King's "I have a dream" speech. The creative power of lighted, inspired words can sound a certain inner note that people recognize and respond to. This then creates dramatic social change. Like King, visionary leaders have the ability to sense the deeper spiritual needs of followers and link their current demands to this deeper, often unspoken need for purpose and meaning.

Sojourner Truth, a former slave, was guided by an inner spiritual experience to preach the emancipation of slaves and women's rights all over the country during the Civil War. President Kwame Nkrumah had a vision to bring independence to Ghana through peace and nonviolence approach.

Visionary leaders transmit energy to people, giving them a new sense of hope and confidence in achieving the vision. Television host Oprah Winfrey helps her guests believe in themselves and work to create a better world.

Visionary leaders often pronounce a vision based on principles that become guidelines for humanity. They intuitively draw on the ageless wisdom and present it in a new synthesis to meet the particular need of the times.

Recommendations about Communication for Effective Change Management

- Communicate regularly, repeatedly, and from multiple channels, including speaking, writing, video, training, focus groups, bulletin boards, Intranets, and more about the change.
- Provide significant amounts of time for people to ask questions, request clarification, and provide input. If you have been part of a scenario in which a leader presented changes, on overhead transparencies, to a large group, and then fled, you know what bad news this is for change integration.
- Clearly communicate the vision, the mission, and the objectives of the change management effort. Help people to understand how these changes will affect them personally. (If you don't help with this process, people will make up their own stories, usually more negative than the truth.)
- Recognize that true communication is a "conversation." It is two-way and real discussion must result. It cannot be just a presentation.
- Provide answers to questions only if you know the answer. Leaders destroy their credibility when they provide incorrect information or appear to stumble or back-peddle, when providing an answer. It is

- much better to say you don't know, and that you will try to find out.
- Leaders need to listen. Avoid defensiveness, excuse-making, and answers that are given too quickly. Act with thoughtfulness.

Leadership:

Leaders aren't born with the phenomenal breadth and scope of thinking that characterizes successful leaders of big companies. Those with a drive to constantly search for more information and see things from a broader view have the potential for it. Drive and aggression are common criteria for identifying leaders and are conveniently easy to observe even in very young people. Leaders must also be able to make sense of all they take in and set a clear course of action. After gathering information from multiple sources and shaping several alternatives, they have to be able to sort out what is important, make a decision, and act on it. Even at lower levels, information is often muddled and the right path is often unclear, but leaders with high potential find clarity and act decisively despite the uncertainty and ambiguity that stymies others. They take disparate facts and observations and connect the dots to create a clear view of what they think is likely to happen before it actually does. Because they see the hazy outlines of change coming before others do, they put their businesses on the offensive.

Another sure sign of a high-potential leader, and one that is especially important in today's environment of tumultuous change, is the leader's passionate quest to continually learn and grow. High potentials seize the opportunity to take "stretch" assignments that tax their abilities precisely because they are stimulated by the challenge and the opportunity to increase their knowledge base about the business, people, and the external world.

Innovative, Courageous Action

Visionaries are especially noted for transforming old mental maps or paradigms, and creating strategies that are "outside the box" of conventional thought. Their thinking is broad and sees the big picture, the whole system. They then create innovative strategies for actualizing their vision. CNN founder Ted Turner transformed television news by boldly creating an around-the-clock international news network.

Visionary leaders anticipate change and are proactive, rather than reactive to events. Their focus is on opportunities, not on problems.

When we see a truly visionary leader accomplishing great things, he is drawing on the resources of their soul and its remarkable capabilities. Each of us can access our inner resources to become a more effective leader in our own field. First we must be willing to take initiative and stand for something we believe in passionately. We must be ready to take the heat. Many of us avoid the responsibility of leadership primarily because we are too sensitive to criticism. But when we know who we truly are and we live from an inner core of values, criticism can be filtered to take in only what is true and helpful to our growth.

Today, as we enter the Third Millennium, thousands of new visionary leaders are emerging in all fields of human endeavor around the world, leading a quiet revolution energized by power of the spirit. By appreciating and supporting those who lead from their core spiritual values, we strengthen those leadership qualities in ourselves.

Four ways to look at what a vision is:

1. A vision is a clear, easily understood and challenging picture of the future of an organization or ministry. People will not act on information they do not understand and there is no vision if people cannot understand it. A vision therefore is clear when those who are a part of the ministry understand it well enough to articulate it to someone else. If the people look puzzled or stammer and stutter, then your vision is obtuse and in need of clarity.
2. A vision is challenging and leaders must know that if they themselves are not challenged by the final product, then the other people in the organization will not be challenged either.
3. A vision is a mental picture, seeing word. A good vision probes the imagination in such a way that it conjures up visual representations in the mind. It is an act of seeing, an imaginative perception of things, combining insight and foresight. Visionaries have the innate ability to see what others do not see. While they see needs, they have the natural capacity to see beyond those needs to the unique, exciting opportunities. For example, Moses led the people of God in the wilderness with a picture in his mind of Israel living

and serving God in a promised land "flowing with milk and honey"
4. A vision is always cast in terms of the future. It is a mental picture of what tomorrow will look like. It is a view of an organization or ministry's future and its exciting possibilities. Visionary leaders spend a large proportion of time thinking about and living in the future. In doing so, they largely determine their future. By cultivating institutional vision, leaders have a vital part in inventing and influencing the future of their organization. They know precisely what they want and where they are going. They press on toward the accomplishment of their goals. However, this does not mean that visionaries ignore either the present or the past. They often use the present as a platform to launch their organization into the future.

Vision has two folds:

- Short term visions – are eventually realized
- Long – term visions are in a constant state of becoming

Moses saw the vision that God gave to him clearly and communicated it to the people in Deuteronomy.

> [7] *For the LORD thy God bringeth thee into a good land, a land of brooks of water, of fountains and depths that spring out of valleys and hills,* [8] *a land of wheat, and barley, and vines, and fig trees, and pomegranates, a land of olive oil, and honey, a land wherein thou shalt eat bread without scarceness. Thou shalt not lack any thing in it; a land whose stones are iron and out of whose hills thou mayest dig brass. (Deuteronomy 8:7-9)*

A vision can be big:

A good vision has potential. A visionary must see big and think big and must know where he or she is going. Also a visionary must think and ask

God for big things as Paul told the people in Ephesus when he was preaching.

> *"Now to Him who is able to do exceeding abundantly beyond all that we ask or think"* (Eph. 3:20)

On the other hand, the vision may be too big, so vast that it tends to overwhelm the visionary. He feels intimidated and defeated just listening to the vision. Others who initially pursue a vision that is too big later become disillusioned and discouraged with the organization or ministry.

A vision grabs hold and won't let go. Not only does the visionary believe that it can be, he is convinced that it must be. He is so gripped by the vision that his spirit refuses to rest until the organization or ministry is moving in the direction of the vision. One is of the believe that God is in it, He is the motivating force behind what the visionary wants to accomplish. There is little question that God has placed the vision on his heart as Nehemiah confirmed.

> *[12] And I arose in the night, I and some few men with me. Neither told I any man what my God had put in my heart to do at Jerusalem; neither was there any beast with me, except the beast that I rode upon.* Nehemiah 2:12

A vision must be because God has chosen to accomplish this vision through this particular person. Perhaps God will use other leaders as well, but this person is convinced that God will use him in a major role, just as God used King David to serve his divine purpose in David's generation

> *[36] For David, after he had served his own generation by the will of God, fell asleep and was laid with his fathers, and saw corruption.* Acts 13:36

The vision audit

We can use the definition of a vision to audit our vision and determine if it meets the criteria of a good vision statement.
As visions are developed, they must be revisited later by these questions:
- *Is my vision clear:* do the people in my ministry understand it?
- *Is it challenging:* does it move my people to action?
- *Does it create a picture:* can they see it in their head?
- *Is it future oriented:* does it present a picture of the organization or ministry's future?
- *Do I believe that it can be:* is it feasible?
- *Am I convinced that it must be:* am I passionate about it?

These practical things are very important about a vision:
- Does your ministry or organization have a vision statement? If the answer is no, why not? How has this affected the organization or ministry?
- How would a clear, challenging vision help the organization or ministry?
- If your organization or church ministry has a vision statement, what is it?
- Is it a short –term or a long –term vision?
- What do you see in your vision? Who make up the vision is of several critical concepts that have a great impact on an organization. Vision is crucial to any organization or ministry. Without vision it is like a surgeon without a scalpel, a cowboy who has lost his horse or a carpenter with a broken hammer. To attempt a ministry without a clear, well-articulated vision is to invite miscarriage.

Habakkuk 2: 2-4

> [2] *And the* LORD *answered me and said: "Write the vision and make it plain upon tablets, that he may run that readeth it.* [3] *For the vision is yet for an appointed time, but at the end it shall speak and not lie. Though it tarry, wait for it, because it will surely come; it*

> *will not tarry. ⁴ Behold, his soul which is lifted up is not upright in him; but the just shall live by his faith.*

Organization vision is clear and challenging, therefore getting a word from God is where organization or ministry begins.

Leadership Vision

Leaders have vision. They share a dream and direction that other people want to share and follow. The leadership vision goes beyond your written organizational mission statement and your vision statement. The vision of leadership permeates the workplace and is manifested in the actions, beliefs, values and goals of your organization's leaders. The vision must:

- Clearly set organizational direction and purpose.
- Inspire loyalty and caring through the involvement of all employees.
- Display and reflect the unique strengths, culture, values, beliefs and direction of the organization.
- Inspire enthusiasm, belief, commitment and excitement in company members.
- Help employees believe that they are part of something bigger than themselves and their daily work.
- Be regularly communicated and shared.
- Challenge people to outdo themselves, to stretch and reach.

The leadership vision is powerful because the senior managers and leaders believe in the vision and mission. Not just a statement hanging on a wall, the leadership vision is even more powerful because people live the leadership vision every single day at work. Employees are not just processing wireless devices to make money for company owners; they are saving the tiniest babies or providing a safe haven for abused women. Can a vision get any more powerful than this?

"The very essence of leadership is that you have to have a vision. It's got to be a vision you articulate clearly and forcefully on every occasion." –Theodore Hesburgh, President of the University of Notre Dame.

"There's nothing more demoralizing than a leader who can't clearly articulate why we're doing what we're doing." –James Kouzes and Barry Posner Habit 2: Begin with the End in Mind.

"Develop a clear definition of what is and is not important to you and your organization. Shape your own future instead of leaving it to the outside influences of other people or circumstances" Stephen R. Covey, 7 habits of highly effective people.

VII. CHAPTER SEVEN
A. MAKING YOUR VISION A REALITY

"To create a world of a strong vision takes courage" (Dr. Akosuah Appiah Sumney)

This vision that you have embarked on is your personality. It is the demonstration of personal choices and the decision to implement a personal idea rather than other people's ideas. Anyone who will encounter you for the first time, will realize that this is the implementation of the illustrator's vision through the demonstration of his style, ideas and personality. Interestingly, one can tell that choices made by a specific leader are radically different from the choices of other visionaries even in regards to the same subject. What is surprising is the unabashed display of this visionaries' personality through his or her work. This work shows in the original visionaries' work, unless of course someone copies it, but then it would be nothing more than a copy and not an original vision. The outcome of vision implemented in a work is a new and different way of looking at the world. It is the creation of a new reality, of a new world. It is in this world that the visionary invites his audience. It is in the reality created by the visionary that the audience is asked to step in. Once inside, the audience is shown the specifics of this world, the details if you will.

The experience, if successful, is complete and will leave the audience speechless and asking for more. Passion has streamed from the visionary towards the audience. Excitement has been shared, and now the desire to experience this world is shared by both the visionary and his audience. Indeed, the trademark of cutting-edge vision is to challenge convention to the creation of a new reality. A number of people are going to find the unconventional approach a welcome respite from the conventional. Those are the people who find the conventional unsatisfying, boring to some extent, commonplace maybe, and definitely not satisfying to them and not fulfilling of their needs. These people seek something else. They seek a different view of the world; a different approach, a different definition of the products, creation and ways of thinking that they are interested in. In other words, they are not only ready for an unconventional approach: they are looking for it. These people are your audience.

B. PERFORMING THE WORK

"If the vision is strong enough, and your goals are stable, and you believe in it, you will bring other people with you". (Dr. Akosuah Appiah Sumney)

The work activates after you have decided to develop your personal vision. Part of this work involves reflecting critically upon what your vision is. The other part of it consists of physically creating work that expresses the vision you defined as the result of your critical thinking. For example, if it's a school, the building must be acquired or constructed.
The goal eventually is to create what I would call a developing vision, meaning a vision that is not superficial but deep rooted. A vision that is meaningful to both the dreamer and his audience. A vision that in a word, is seen and can be touched.

To do so the two parts of this process; reflecting upon your vision and creating new development based on the outcome of your reflection, must be brought together. In practice, the two parts of this process are not really separate. Instead, they are intertwined. Critical thinking leads to the creation of new work and this new work in turn leads to further critical thinking. It is an interactive process that on the one hand consists of reflection and on the other hand consists of creating new ideas for the vision. At times the two take place simultaneously. This occurs for example in the field when the sight of a new subject leads to new ideas that are immediately developed into the creation of the vision.
The critical thinking aspect of your work does not need to take place only in your mind. Instead, I recommend you write down the thoughts, the ideas and the insights that your Imagination brings. You can also use a voice recorder to preserve your thoughts, a process that some prefer because they want it to be faster than writing.
Whatever approach you prefer I do recommend that you engage in a recorded description of your vision. Remember that, as we saw previously, vision is something that at first exists in your mind's eye. Remember that vision is immaterial and known only to you until it is interpreted into a medium that you can share with others. Writing or audio recordings represent such a medium. Once you have written or recorded an audio description of your vision, you can share this description with others, either in print or in oral form. You can either print it, read it or play the audio. At any rate this vision is no longer something that exists only in

your mind. It is something that has been formulated as a text. In effect, although this may not be your goal, it is now literature.

Nevertheless, having a written description of what your vision is, what you want to express, and of what you want your audience to know, can only be helpful as a road map to guide you and your team as a blueprint for your upcoming work.

VIII. CHAPTER EIGHT
A. DO NOT ABANDON YOUR VISION

The real tragedy in life is not death but what dies in us though we are still alive.

The fact of the matter is that you will not find your vision by attempting to work with a subject that is not yours. You will not express the fullness of your vision working with a subject that you do not love or that you are not excited about. You must be creating what you love and what you are passionate about for your vision to fully express itself and become a reality.

There is a difference between liking something and loving something. For example, I like to travel a lot but I don't have passion of visiting museums. Changing the vision is a hard thing to do, and should not be undertaken lightly. Don't change the vision, rather you can change the direction of the vision.

So how do you know it's time to change direction? And how do you pick a new direction? These are challenging questions. You have to go back to the drawing board again where you began and follow the trend to see what has worked and what has not worked. You can change some of these dynamics from your findings.

Don't Abandon Your Vision, Expect Results.

Through writing down your goals, using the power of visualization and imagination, you can achieve **remarkable results**. Visualization and imagination allow you to **change your beliefs, assumptions**, and **opinions** about the most important person in your life, YOU! They allow you to connect to your brain cells and get them all working in a singular and purposeful direction.

Your subconscious will become engaged in a process that transforms you forever. The process is invisible and doesn't take a long time. It just happens over time, as long as you put in the time to visualize and affirm, surround yourself with positive people, read uplifting books and listen to audio programs that flood your mind with positive, life-affirming messages.

The cause of many visions failures is not poor planning or lack of appropriate skills. It is quite simply the absence of a clear vision. When

thinking about your vision, use the acronym ACCH - Achievable, Comprehensible, Controllable and Helpful, to help you. Meditate extensively and firm about why you are doing what you are doing.
Ask your customer to help you define success measures for the project.

B. VISION AUGMENTATION

1 - Define your vision in writing or in recordings.
Consider this exercise as experimental. Approach it as a brainstorming session. Keep in mind that no one else but you will see this writing or hear this recording. You do not have to share it with anyone unless you wish to. Write down as many ideas and as many things about your vision as they come to you. Do not revise, do not erase, and do not correct typos. This is not a Ph.D. dissertation. This is just to help you find out where you want to go with your work.
There is no right or wrong. You can sort things out after you are completed. Do not stop writing until you have written everything you want to write.
I recommend you do this exercise in a place where there are no distractions. Make sure to turn off the phone, so that you will not be interrupted in anyway.

2 – Describe the kind of projects you've always wanted to create.
Describe the kind of projects you've always wanted to create. Also describe the projects you are presently creating. Is there a difference between the two? If yes describe what this difference is. Secondly, set small and realistic daily goals to move you towards your major project. Human brains are extremely adaptive. The only way to re-wire your brain to identify itself with success is by collecting small successes. Set small and achievable projects so that each time you complete a project and succeed you send success signals to your brain. And in no time, your brain reprograms and re-tunes itself for success, having memorized various recent success patterns. This then makes you feel better about yourself. You become happier and have more energy to keep advancing.

Lack of clear vision: This is where everything begins. If you do not know what exactly you want, you will live your entire life being controlled by the opinions of others. Lack of clear direction in life alone generates a tremendous amount of stress and anxiety.

Every human contains a powerful success mechanism, which is goal-striving. It only becomes activated when a clear goal is in view. So sit down and decide what you really want to accomplish. Do not borrow another person's dream. Set your life goal and believe in its possibility. If you are not passionate and convinced enough about where you are going in life, someone else will succeed in convincing you to look the other way. You may have already got a clear vision. That is great! Never stop visualizing its completion in your mind. And keep advancing in the right direction daily, no matter how small the step you are taking may be.

IX. CHAPTER NINE
A. CONCLUSION

As a visionary your heart must be into your work. When it comes to developing your vision, this vision must reflect what is in your heart. One thing that I learned many years ago is that it is not possible to have a good vision if your heart is not in it. Even if you try to do so your audience eventually will see that you are not totally involved and people will eventually distance themselves from your work as a result.

A vision can be successful when it demonstrates your passion, your personality and your visualization. If you are not passionate about your work, if your heart is not in it, your audience will be able to tell.

For your vision to be unique it has to be implemented through a style unique to you, a personal style. All these will play out and you can achieve your personal style without conforming to the norm.

B. POLITICAL TRANFORMATIONAL LEADERSHIP

Political leaders are supposed to be transformational leaders who can empower others. Political leaders who should form part of transformational leadership must encourage the masses not just to vote for them for popularity. Political leaders must change from theory to practical political leaders who have a clear strategy for turning political visions into reality. Through methodical, analytical, political, and emotional intelligence, leaders chart paths to promising futures that include economic growth, material prosperity, and human security. Unfortunately, such leaders are rare in the world. Often foundations are fragile and greed, corruption and exploitation are in abundance. Accountable leadership therefore has the potential to influence the greatest change through their immeasurable visions.

So can our political leaders guide us toward a safer world?
Political transformational leaders must be prepared to put forward long-term plans for decades, even centuries, to assist the growth and development of a nation. They must work on appealing to both the immediate and long term development of their nations.

Political transformational leaders know how to give power away and how to make others feel powerful. They give followers access to the funding, materials, authority and information needed to complete tasks and develop new ideas. This allows others to make decisions instead of making all the decisions by themselves.

Political transformational leaders are more effective than powerful political leaders.
Such leaders are:
- Creative
- Collaborative
- Idealistic
- Empowering
- Compassionate
- Loving

The finest and best effective political leaders are able to paint a captivating and inspiring picture of what the future will look like. This imagery can inspire others to work with them toward a strong structured vision. Their visions are detailed, graphic and believed to be attainable by those who choose to follow them. The evidence is simple: true leaders' visualize the future in their mind's eye and then effectively communicate that future to their prospective investors, employees, vendors and clients. It takes a great political visionary leader to direct people and the businesses in their nations to success. Whether they led a constituency, cities or a country, history's paramount political leaders understood the importance of providing the motivation and direction to achieve larger goals.

Secondly, the political transformational visionary leader is skillful in designing and creating an organizational culture which will make promising the accomplishment of the leader's vision and ideas. Creating this organizational culture is the most long-lasting contribution of the leader's values, vision and beliefs that are shared by members of the union. Every charismatic political leader is able to instill in others the ideas, beliefs and values of the vision so that they become empowered to make the vision their own. The political transformational visionary leader must have a vision into the far future that, can develop an effective organization and can attract others. Another characteristic of a truly effective leader is that she/he always focuses simultaneously on two seemingly different configurations, yet to such a leader they are always inextricably related, such as:
Visionary transformational leaders in politics often are capable to capture the desires of the public.

Government and Politician's role in society should be to make policies and decisions that target the social and economic wellbeing of people and society as a whole. Decisions by people in office of power that impact only a very small section of the society in my view are not always the best decisions. The "vision" is not something all great leaders have. It was seen throughout history in the great ones. For example, Alexander the Great obviously had a vision of how to make an empire work. Visionary has many different essentials to it.

It's surprising how few leaders really have a strong view of what is happening socially or economically in their industry, nation or globally. In one respect, you might say they are blind. Leaders need a vision, but great transformational leadership turns that vision into reality. So remember each political transformational leader with a vision will inculcate these steps:
  a. Strategy and tactics
  b. Goals and objectives
  c. Big picture ideas and little picture details
  d. Statesman and politician
  e. Profound and practical
  f. Architect and plumber
  g. Wisdom and application
  h. Futuristic ideas and present actions

Political, Governmental Transformational Leadership

Transformational leaders generate something new from something old by changing the simple political and cultural structures. This differs from the political leaders who make modifications to the organizational mission, structure, and human resources.

Political transformational leadership accomplishes this by stimulating and renovating people's emotions, values, ethics, standards, and long-term goals through the process of charismatic and visionary leadership.

The term "Transformational Leadership" was first coined by Downton (1973), however, its emergence did not really come about until James Burn's classic, Leadership (1978), was published. Burn noted that the majority of leadership models and practices were based on transactional processes that focused on exchanges between the leader and followers, such as promotions for performing excellent work or punishment for being late. On the other hand, transformational leaders engage with their followers to create a connection that raises the level of motivation and morality in not only the followers, but also the leaders themselves.

C. LEADERSHIP AND ORGANIZATIONAL VISION.

"All leaders have the capacity to create a compelling vision, one that takes people to an innovative place, and the ability to translate that vision into reality". Leadership must demonstrate characteristics as the vision holder, the guardian of the dream, or the person who has a vision of the organization's purpose. The first obligation of a leader is to define "Reality". Leaders "manage the imagination".
"Visionary Leadership" is very important.

There are four different areas to look at regarding this development.

1. Organization
2. Future
3. Personal
4. Strategic

Organizational vision involves having a complete picture of a system's components as well as an understanding of their interrelationships. "Future vision is a comprehensive picture of how an organization will look at some point in the future, including how it will be positioned in its environment and how it will function internally" (Manasse, 1986, p. 157). Personal vision includes the leader's personal aspirations for the organization and acts as the impetus for the leader's actions that will link organizational and future vision. "Strategic vision involves connecting the reality of the present (organizational vision) to the possibilities of the future (future vision) in a unique way (personal vision) that is appropriate for the organization and its leader" (Manasse, 1986, p. 162). A leader's vision needs to be shared by those who will be involved in the realization of the vision.

D. WISE SAYINGS BY DR. AKOSUAH APPIAH SUMNEY

- ❖ A good vision compels Leadership to put oneself at risk
- ❖ A good vision is the dream made into reality
- ❖ A good vision will take people to the top
- ❖ A good vision is what good leaders ensure
- ❖ No good leader grows to the top alone
- ❖ People functioning together for a corporate vision is an incredible experience
- ❖ No matter how big your dream is, dream bigger!
- ❖ Best visionaries are listeners
- ❖ Discover your unique vision and motivate yourself to make it a reality
- ❖ No matter how hard and strong a good vision is, not everyone will follow it
- ❖ Everything increases or decreases depending on the leadership vision
- ❖ To see how well the political leader is doing, look at the results in the nation
- ❖ A good vision brings following
- ❖ A good vision changes the people
- ❖ A good vision grows the environment

BIBLIOGRAPHY

1. Bennis, W. *The 4 competencies of leadership. Training and Development Journal*, (1984 15-19).

2. Covey, Stephen, *The 7 Habits of Highly Effective People* (New York: Simon & Shuster, 1989).

3. Drucker, Peter, *Managing the Non-Profit Organization:* (New York: Harper Business, 1990).

4. Herrington, Bonem, and Furr, Leading congregational change: (Library of Congress Cataloging, 2000).

5. Jewish Bible.

6. Kouzes and Posner, *The leadership challenge:* (by Jossey-Bass 1987).

7. Manasse, A. L. *Vision and leadership:* (Peabody Journal of Education, 150-173 1986).

8. Malphurs, Aubrey, *Developing a vision for Ministry in the 21st. Century:* (Grand Rapids: Baker Book House 1974).

9. Malphurs, Aubrey, *Values-Driven Leadership:* (Grand Rapids: Baker Book House, 1996).

10. Malphurs, Aubrey, *Strategy 2000:* (Grand Rapids: Kregel Publications, 1996).

11. New King James Bible.

12. Warren, Bennis, *Managing the Dream:* (Basic Books, 2000).

13. Warren, Bennis *Leadership in the 21st Century:* (Basic Books. Bennis 1990).

14. Stewart 1991.
15. Westley, F. & Mintzberg H, Visionary Leadership & Strategic Management, Journal (Volume 10, 1989).